FLAVOURS OF ENGLAND

VEGETARIAN

GILLI DAVIES AND HUW JONES

GRAFFEG

Flavours of England: Vegetarian
Published in Great Britain in 2019 by
Graffeg Limited

Text by Gilli Davies copyright © 2019.
Photographs by Huw Jones copyright © 2019.
Food styling by Adam Whittle.
Designed and produced by Graffeg Limited
copyright © 2019.

Graffeg Limited, 24 Stradey Park Business
Centre, Mwrwg Road, Llangennech, Llanelli,
Carmarthenshire SA14 8YP Wales UK
Tel 01554 824000 www.graffeg.com

Gilli Davies is hereby identified as the author of
this work in accordance with section 77 of the
Copyrights, Designs and Patents Act 1988.

A CIP Catalogue record for this book is
available from the British Library.

ISBN 9781912654772

1 2 3 4 5 6 7 8 9

CONTENTS

Vegetarian

When it comes to strange names for culinary dishes, the English can boast a few.

Pan Haggerty is one example, a traditional Northumbrian dish of potatoes and onions flavoured with cheese. But perhaps it's Bubble & Squeak that takes your fancy? A traditional breakfast dish, it gets its name from the cabbage which makes bubbling and squeaking sounds during cooking.

On the more conventional front, just find a good quality English greengrocer to create delicious and unusual vegetarian dishes, the best of which may be the leek and cheese sausage. With a harvest of fresh beans, peas, carrots and courgettes, you have all the ingredients to make a rich terrine of vegetables that looks great too.

Using carrots again, make up a flan, wrapping the mixture in large spinach leaves for maximum flavour and effect.

It could be that an asparagus and pecorino risotto takes your fancy, or a roast squash salad with feta cheese and toasted seeds, but then again some of the most popular pub foods in England at the moment are a good vegetarian curry or mac 'n' cheese.

VEGETABLE TERRINE

This is a deliciously rich mixture of vegetables that looks extremely pretty too.

VEGETABLE TERRINE

Ingredients

350g carrots, peeled and roughly chopped

150ml crème fraîche

25g butter

50g cream cheese

1 tablespoon lemon juice

2 eggs

350g green vegetables: beans, peas, courgettes, etc.

Salt and ground black pepper

Serves 6

1 Pre-heat the oven to 180°C/350°F/Gas 4.

2 Cook the carrots gently with the crème fraîche and butter until soft. Liquidize and cool before adding the seasoning, cream cheese, eggs and lemon juice.

3 Prepare the green vegetables by cutting into appropriate-sized pieces and blanching.

4 Line a loaf tin with cling film or foil. Layer the carrot puree with the different vegetables to make an attractive dish.

5 Cover and seal the top with foil. Cook for 30 minutes in a bain marie, or use a large baking tin with enough water in it to come halfway up the loaf tin.

6 Serve chilled, cut into slices.

CARROT AND SPINACH FLAN

This is a very colourful dish and full of flavour, with the sweet carrot filling surrounded by the strong flavour of the spinach leaves.

CARROT AND SPINACH FLAN

Ingredients

1 head of spring greens or 12 largish fresh spinach leaves

225g carrots, peeled and grated

1 medium onion, finely chopped

15g butter

1 egg

2 tablespoons double cream

Pinch of ground cumin

Salt and ground black pepper

Serves 4

1 Pre-heat the oven to 180°C/350°F/Gas 4.

2 Blanch the spring greens/spinach leaves in a pan of boiling water then plunge into cold water to retain the bright green colour.

3 Cut off the stems and any strong veins in the leaves then use them to line a 15cm flan dish, overlapping, and leaving enough of the leaves flopping outside the dish to fold back over once the filling is in place.

4 Fry the onion in the butter until soft but not brown. Beat the egg, cream, cumin and seasoning together, then add the cooked onion and grated carrot and mix well.

5 Spoon the mixture into the lined flan dish, cover with the overlapping greens and wrap the whole dish in foil.

6 Place the wrapped flan dish in a roasting tray with enough water to come halfway up the side of the flan dish. Bake in the oven for 45 minutes.

7 Turn the carrot flan out of the dish, cut into four wedges and serve.

PAN HAGGERTY

This is a traditional Northumbrian dish of potatoes and onions flavoured with cheese. It's good on its own or as part of a meal.

PAN HAGGERTY

Ingredients

75g butter

1kg floury potatoes, such as King Edwards, peeled and cut into 5-6mm slices

500g onions, thinly sliced

225g well-flavoured hard cheese, such as cheddar, coarsely grated

Serves 4-6

1 Pre-heat the oven to 200°C/400°F/Gas 6.

2 Bring a large pan of salted water to the boil. Add the potatoes, then return to the boil and cook for 5-10 minutes until just tender when pierced with a sharp knife. Drain well and set aside.

3 In a large frying pan, melt 50g butter. Add the sliced onions, season well, then cook gently for about 20 minutes until soft and lightly browned. Remove and keep warm.

4 Using the remaining butter, cook the potatoes a few slices at a time in the frying pan until crisp and golden underneath.

5 Arrange 1/3 of the potatoes in the bottom of an ovenproof dish, then cover with half of the cooked onions, a little seasoning and a third of the cheese.

6 Add a second layer of potatoes and the remaining onions. Season, then scatter over half of the remaining cheese.

7 Add a final layer of potatoes, then scatter the remaining grated cheese.

8 Bake in the oven for 20-25 minutes until golden.

BUBBLE & SQUEAK

It's the bits of potato that catch in the pan that define the term 'bubble and squeak', so be brave and continue to cook until you can smell a slight singeing and a delicious aroma coming from the underside of your potato cake.

BUBBLE & SQUEAK

Ingredients

50g butter

1 onion, finely sliced

1 garlic clove, chopped

15-20 cooked Brussel sprouts

Sliced or leftover cooked cabbage, shredded

400g cold leftover mashed potato

Salt and ground black pepper

Serves 4-6

❶ Melt the butter in a large non-stick frying pan and cook the onion and garlic gently for about 5 minutes, until soft but not brown.

❷ Add the sliced sprouts or cabbage, toss to heat through and let it colour slightly.

❸ Add the mashed potato and fold into the other ingredients, adding lots of salt and pepper.

❹ Press down on the mixture so that it covers the base of the pan and forms a large, flattish cake. Allow the mixture to catch slightly on the base of the pan before turning it over and doing the same again.

❺ Cut into wedges and serve.

SPINACH, STILTON, CELERY AND WALNUT FILO RING

This makes a spectacular dish and could be used for a celebration, such as Christmas or a birthday party.

SPINACH, STILTON, CELERY AND WALNUT FILO RING

Ingredients

1kg frozen leaf spinach, thawed and squeezed dry

1 bunch of spring onions, finely sliced

2 eggs, beaten together

Salt and ground black pepper

100g stilton, crumbled

4 sticks celery, chopped

100g walnuts, chopped

8 sheets filo pastry

50g melted butter

Serves 6

1 Pre-heat the oven to 200°C/400°F/Gas 6.

2 Mix the spinach with the spring onions, eggs and seasoning.

3 Mix the stilton with the celery and walnuts.

4 Brush 3 sheets of filo with butter and stack them on top of each other. Arrange half of the spinach mixture over the top 2/3 of the pastry. Spread the stilton mixture on top and roll the filo into a sausage shape.

5 Brush another 3 sheets of filo with butter and fill in the same manner.

6 Shape both filo sausages into half circles and join together to make a ring. Fold the remaining sheets of filo to give a quadruple thickness and cut out holly leaves or stars.

7 Brush the ring with the remaining melted butter and decorate with the leaves.

8 Bake for 30-35 minutes, until golden.

BROCCOLI AND GOATS' CHEESE TART

This is a very pretty tart, particularly when cut so that the layer of tomato puree shows across the bottom of the filling.

BROCCOLI AND GOATS' CHEESE TART

Ingredients

225g shortcrust pastry

200g purple sprouting broccoli

100g soft fresh goats' cheese, crumbled

2 tablespoons spicy tomato chutney

2 eggs

2 egg yolks

300ml full-fat milk

Salt and ground black pepper

Serves 4-6

1 Preheat the oven to 220°C/425°F/Gas 7.

2 Make up or buy the pastry.

3 Roll it out thinly and line a 25cm flan tin.

4 Spread the tomato chutney over the base of the pastry then arrange the broccoli spears in a circle with their stems pointing to the centre.

5 Beat the eggs, egg yolks, crumbled goats' cheese and milk together. Season very well (an egg and milk mixture can be very bland).

6 Put the flan tin on a baking sheet and bake the tart for 10 minutes to set the pastry, then turn the heat down to 200°C/400°F/Gas 6 and continue to cook for another 20-25 minutes, until golden brown on top.

7 Serve warm with a tomato and red onion salad.

VEGETABLE CURRY

Although curry is an Indian dish modified for British tastes, it's so popular that each October the English celebrate a national curry week.

A recipe for curry was first published in The Art of Cookery Made Plain & Easy by Hannah Glasse in 1747, but curry was served in the Norris Street Coffee House in Haymarket as early as 1733. By 1784, curry and rice had become specialties in some popular restaurants in the area around London's Piccadilly.

VEGETABLE CURRY

Ingredients

1 tablespoon olive oil

2 red onions, thinly sliced

175g jalfrezi curry paste

1 small butternut squash, peeled and cut into chunks

1 small cauliflower, broken into florets

1 vegetable stock cube

1 bunch coriander, stalked and leaves finely chopped

500ml passata

1 red pepper, sliced

1 yellow pepper, sliced

400g can chickpeas, drained and rinsed

100g natural yoghurt

1 fresh green chilli, finely diced

Boiled rice and naan bread, to serve

Serves 6

1 Heat the oil in a large frying pan. Add the onions and cook over a low heat for about 8-10 minutes until soft.

2 Add the jalfrezi paste and mix well, then add the squash cubes, cauliflower florets, stock cube, coriander stalks, passata and 500ml water. Simmer for 20 minutes, adding some more water if it gets too thick.

3 Add the peppers and chickpeas and cook for another 15-20 minutes, until all the vegetables are tender.

4 Stir in the yoghurt and most of the coriander leaves. Serve scattered with the rest of the coriander and the diced chilli, with rice and naan bread on the side.

ASPARAGUS AND PECORINO RISOTTO

Asparagus grows particularly well around York and now that pecorino is produced in Yorkshire too, this is an excellent combination of local ingredients.

ASPARAGUS AND PECORINO RISOTTO

Ingredients

700g fine asparagus

1 medium onion, chopped

75g butter

320g risotto rice

240ml white wine

800ml light vegetable stock, hot

300g pecorino, grated

Salt and ground black pepper

Serves 4

1 Trim the asparagus, remove the spears and keep to one side and cut the stems into 3cm lengths.

2 Fry the onion in 50g butter over a moderate heat for 10 minutes until soft.

3 Add the rice, fry for 2 minutes more, then pour in the wine and simmer until absorbed.

4 Add the stock a little at a time, waiting for it to be mostly absorbed between additions. Taste for seasoning all the time. About 5 minutes before the end (roughly 10 minutes after you started adding stock), add the asparagus stems.

5 When the rice is still a touch too al dente for you, crumble in three-quarters of the percorino, the asparagus spears and the remaining 25g butter. Cover and leave for 5 minutes.

6 Serve with the remaining pecorino scattered on top.

ROAST SQUASH SALAD WITH FETA CHEESE & TOASTED SEEDS

A delightful salad with mixed flavours and textures. Serve with chunks of fresh bread to make a healthy meal and, if the weather's cold, conjure up a bowl of soup first.

ROAST SQUASH SALAD WITH FETA CHEESE & TOASTED SEEDS

Ingredients

1 butternut squash, peeled, deseeded and chunked (2.5cm)

1 tablespoon olive oil

2 tablespoons sunflower seeds

1 tablespoon linseeds and sesame seeds

A generous handful of wild rocket

200g feta cheese

For the dressing:

3 tablespoons olive oil

1 tablespoon balsamic vinegar

Serves 4-6

1 Roast the squash with the oil at 200°C/400°F/Gas 6 for about 20 minutes. Leave to cool.

2 Toast the seeds in a heavy-based frying pan.

3 Make up the dressing.

4 Arrange the squash and rocket in a serving dish, scatter over the feta and seeds and pour over the dressing.

MAC 'N' CHEESE

This is high fashion with English pub diners right now. It combines the family favourite dish of pasta with a rich cheesy sauce made from any one of the excellent range of English cheddars available.

MAC 'N' CHEESE

Ingredients

350g tube, spiral or other short and chunky pasta

2 tablespoons butter

3 tablespoons plain flour

1 teaspoon English mustard

500ml whole milk

250g vegetarian mature cheddar, grated

50g Parmesan, grated

Salt and ground black pepper

Crisp breadcrumbs made from 2 slices of bread, spread with butter, crisped in a hot oven for 10 minutes then crumbled

Serves 4

1. Heat the oven to 200°C/400°F/Gas 6.

2. Boil the pasta until just cooked.

3. Melt the butter in a good-sized saucepan and then stir in the flour and mustard. Continue to cook for a minute before whisking in all the milk.

4. Continue whisking over the heat until the sauce thickens and becomes smooth, then simmer for 3 minutes.

5. Take off the heat, stir in all of the cheddar and half of the Parmesan.

6. Stir the pasta and some seasoning into the cheesy sauce. Tip into a large ovenproof dish, or 4 individual dishes.

7. Scatter over the breadcrumbs and the remaining Parmesan then bake for 20 minutes until crisp and golden.

METRIC AND IMPERIAL EQUIVALENTS

Weights	Solid
15g	½oz
25g	1oz
40g	1½oz
50g	1¾oz
75g	2¾oz
100g	3½oz
125g	4½oz
150g	5½oz
175g	6oz
200g	7oz
250g	9oz
300g	10½oz
400g	14oz
500g	1lb 2oz
1kg	2lb 4oz
1.5kg	3lb 5oz
2kg	4lb 8oz
3kg	6lb 8oz

Volume	Liquid
15ml	½ floz
30ml	1 floz
50ml	2 floz
100ml	3½ floz
125ml	4 floz
150ml	5 floz (¼ pint)
200ml	7 floz
250ml	9 floz
300ml	10 floz (½ pint)
400ml	14 floz
450ml	16 floz
500ml	18 floz
600ml	1 pint (20 floz)
1 litre	1¾ pints
1.2 litre	2 pints
1.5 litre	2¾ pints
2 litres	3½ pints
3 litres	5¼ pints

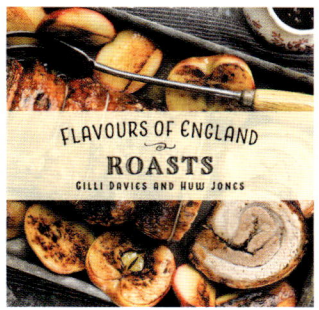

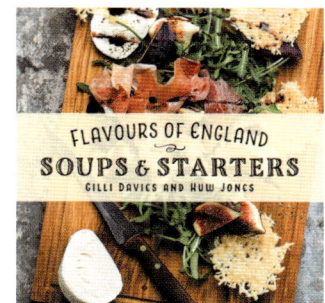

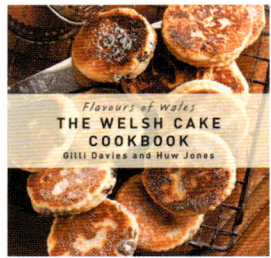

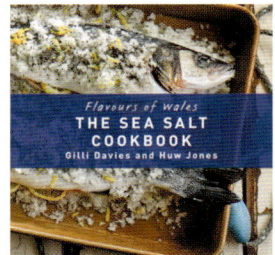
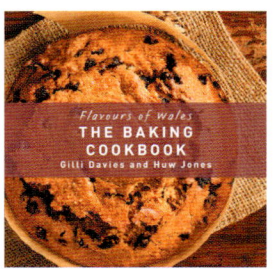